# ⊙ EATING THE PLATES ⊙

*A child posing
with her cat.*

# •EATING•
# THE PLATES:

## *A Pilgrim Book of Food and Manners*

BY Lucille Recht Penner

❋

WITH ILLUSTRATIONS

SELECTED BY THE AUTHOR

SCHOLASTIC INC.
New York Toronto London Auckland Sydney

ISBN 0-590-46975-4

12 11 10 9 8 7 6                                                                    9/9012/0

Printed in the U.S.A.                                                                      **23**

First Scholastic printing, November 1993

*To my father-in-law*

# •Contents•

# ✸ EATING THE PLATES ✸

# Introduction:

## Good-bye Forever

✷

My country, 'tis of thee
Sweet land of liberty,
   Of thee I sing:
Land where my fathers died,
Land of the pilgrim's pride,
From every mountain side
   Let freedom ring.

—Samuel Francis Smith,
"America"

*T*his book is about the eating habits, customs, and manners of real people who lived a long time ago.

We call them the **Pilgrims.** Pilgrims are people who travel to a faraway place in order to pray there.

The Pilgrims were born in England close to four hundred years ago. Back then, English people had to pray the way the king said they should. If they didn't, they could be put in prison or even killed.

The Pilgrims wanted to pray in their own way. So they decided to leave England and find a new home.

First they went to Holland. The people of Holland, called the Dutch, were nice to the Pilgrims. They gave them homes and jobs. Some Pilgrims became weavers, tailors, and button makers. Others became masons and bricklayers.

*The King of England was angry at the Pilgrims. He wanted to put them in jail.*

The Pilgrims were safe in Holland. But they were not happy living among the Dutch. They thought the Dutch were more interested in money and fun than they were in religion. And the Pilgrims were afraid that their children would grow up to be just like the Dutch.

So they decided to take a big chance—to sail across the ocean to America.

It was a very dangerous and very scary thing to do.

Only a few English people had been to America. Many still believed that the earth was flat. They thought that if you sailed too far you would fall off the edge.

Even people who knew that the earth was round were worried. What was America like? Was it safe there? The Pilgrims were afraid. But they made up their minds to go.

First they needed supplies—a *lot* of supplies. There wouldn't be any stores in America! They had to bring with them everything they would need when they got there: clothes and shoes and dishes and furniture, food and drink and weapons and tools, farming equipment, cloth, and beads to trade to the Indians.

To buy all of these supplies, and to hire a ship for the long voyage, would cost a tremendous amount of money. In fact, the trip would cost more money than the Pilgrims had.

So they made a deal with a group of English investors. These investors were called the Merchant Adventurers.

The Merchant Adventurers hired a ship, named the *Mayflower,* to take the Pilgrims to America. And they gave the Pilgrims food and supplies.

In return, the Pilgrims agreed to work for the Merchant Adventurers for seven years. Everything valuable that the Pilgrims found in America—such as animal furs, beautiful bird feathers, oil, and whale ivory—would belong to the investors. The Pilgrims would keep for themselves only things that they needed to stay alive.

The Merchant Adventurers made the same deal with other settlers who were traveling on the *Mayflower.* The Pilgrims called these other settlers "Strangers." The Pilgrims called themselves "Saints."

After the agreement with the Merchant Adventurers was signed, some of the Pilgrims almost changed their minds. They thought their children were too young for such a dangerous trip to an unknown place.

Finally they decided to leave little children and old

people behind with friends. They would send for them after they were settled.

It was sad to say good-bye.

But on September 6, 1620, the time finally came to raise the anchor. Wind was filling the sails. The narrow deck of the *Mayflower* was crowded with crying, waving, shouting Saints and Strangers.

Slowly the *Mayflower* swung about and pointed her prow toward America.

*The Mayflower was
battered by rain and wind.*

# 1

# Bugs for Dinner

❖

You gentlemen of England
That live at home at ease,
Ah! little do you think upon
The danger of the seas.

—Martyn Parker

For sixty-six days the Pilgrims sailed across the Atlantic Ocean.

The wind howled. The waves crashed against the sides of the little, crowded wooden boat. It was always noisy. Inside the boat, people moaned, coughed, and shouted to make themselves heard against the roar of the wind and the creaking of the sails.

They were always cold and wet. Spray from the big ocean waves soaked everything on deck. Soon their clothes became stiff with salt left by the seawater.

There were a hundred and two passengers. Most of them slept crowded together in the main cabin. The ceiling was low. Anyone over five feet tall had to walk bent over.

Each person had only a tiny space in which to sleep, prepare food, eat, wash, and pile all his or her belongings. And everyone had tried to bring enough things to last a lifetime!

Blankets, rugs, pillows, quilts, sheets, furniture, boxes of clothes and linens, dishes, tools, guns, armor, cradles, pots, pans, and special keepsakes were piled up to the ceiling. The cabin was jammed!

It was hard for anyone even to move in there. And it smelled terrible.

Hardly anybody washed—there wasn't enough fresh water. And even people who washed their hands and faces didn't wash their clothes.

Most people never changed at all. They wore the same clothes for the whole trip.

The Saints and Strangers scratched and scratched, because lice and fleas lived in everyone's clothes and hair. There was no way to get rid of them.

Besides human beings and bugs, the *Mayflower* carried other passengers. Live rabbits, chickens, geese, and ducks were kept in a rowboat that was lashed to the deck.

There were also pigs, goats, and sheep on board. But no one got to eat them. The settlers hoped that these few animals would become the parents of large flocks and herds in America.

What *did* the Pilgrims eat during their long voyage?

Most of the food on the *Mayflower* was cold and dry. There were moldy cheese and dried peas. Salty beef and dried fish.

And there were **ship's biscuits**—as hard as rocks. Hundreds of these biscuits had been carried onto the boat before it sailed. They were stacked in huge piles.

Ship's biscuits were made of wheat flour, pea flour, and water. They were flat and round, the size of dinner plates.

The stale biscuits were almost impossible to chew. But somehow people sucked and nibbled them down.

Cheese was different. It didn't get as hard as the biscuits. Instead, the cheese quickly turned green and moldy.

Dried peas were stored in sacks so the mice and rats that dashed all over the ship wouldn't eat them. The settlers ate some of the peas on board, saving the rest to eat when they got to America.

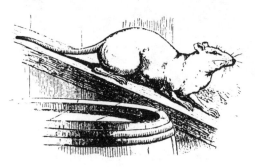

There were also sacks of turnips, parsnips, onions, and cabbages. Vegetables kept pretty well. They just got a little hard on the outside and a little soft on the inside.

Some days the Pilgrims ate smoked herring or dried, salted codfish.

Other days they had pork or beef. Because fresh meat would have spoiled quickly, the Pilgrims' meat was preserved in salt and packed in barrels.

One of their favorite meats was **neat's tongue**—the tongue of an ox. They brought big boxes of dried ox tongues to eat on the trip.

Other boxes held spices—ginger, cinnamon, mace, cloves, nutmeg, and green ginger. These were very expensive, but the Pilgrims loved spicy food. And spices could cover up the bad taste of food that had begun to rot.

To wash down their salty, spicy meals, the Pilgrims drank beer, ale, wine, and even gin and brandy. They hated water. Even children drank beer.

Everyone on the *Mayflower* needed to drink often. When a family crouched around its mattress at meal-time, it was usually looking at cold, dry, salty food.

But sometimes it was better not to look. Rats and cockroaches were all over. Little insects—weevils, maggots, and grubs—chewed tunnels into the ship's biscuits.

Some of the Pilgrims preferred to eat at night. In the dark, they couldn't see the bugs crawling on their food.

✹

Once in a while, each family got a treat: the chance to cook a hot dinner.

Cooking usually wasn't allowed on the *Mayflower*. A stray spark could start a fire that might burn up the whole ship.

But there were three small, iron boxes filled with sand for people to cook in. These were called **fireboxes**. The settlers took turns using them.

Sometimes they made **labscouse**—a thick soup of dried peas mixed with water and chunks of salty beef. The hot soup tasted delicious. And you could dip your hard biscuit into the soup to soften it.

Little fat dumplings, called **doughboys**, were made by frying bits of wet flour in pork fat.

A real treat was **burgoo**—hot oatmeal and molasses. Another was **plum duff.** Duff was a fatty pudding. Plum duff had raisins or dried prunes mixed in.

Hot food was special. Aboard the *Mayflower,* nobody had it often. Usually the Pilgrims ate cold, dry, buggy meals, drank beer, and dreamed of how well they would eat when they finally reached America, the land of plenty.

*The Pilgrims rowed
to shore in a small boat.*

# 2

# A Land of Plenty?

✵

Hunger is the best cook!

—Roman saying

*H*urrah! We're here.
Now we can go off on our own!

That's what a lot of passengers said when they saw land. They were tired of living on a crowded little boat. They were tired of the other families.

The Pilgrim leaders said no.

They said it was important to stick together. Then

they would be able to build strong houses, plant crops, and fight off the Indians if they attacked. If they separated they might all be killed.

Everyone saw that this was true. So they signed an agreement. Today, we call their agreement the Mayflower Compact. It said that they would form a colony with "just and equall lawes for all."

The Mayflower Compact worked. The *Mayflower* passengers stayed together. Now they were all called Pilgrims—the Strangers as well as the Saints. They elected John Carver to be their first governor.

Then they were ready to begin a new life in a new world.

✪

It was a wild place. At night, the howls of wolves drifted across the water from the dark shore. The Pilgrim children stood with their parents on the deck of the *Mayflower* and stared into the blackness.

Soon they saw the tiny glow of a fire. Then another fire. And another. Indians!

Were the Indians watching them? Were they planning to attack?

It was scary, but the Pilgrims had to be brave. They needed fresh food. They needed to find a spot to build their houses. They had to go ashore.

In the morning, some of the men put on the armor they had brought from England. They took their heavy handguns, which were called **muskets**, gunpowder, and food—hard biscuits and cheese.

If the *Mayflower* came too close to the land, it would get stuck in the sand. So the Pilgrim men climbed into a rowboat and rowed toward the beach.

They could hear the waves breaking and see the spray of white foam. When the keel of their boat scraped along the bottom, they got out and waded through the cold water. At last they stood, shivering, on the American shore.

The Pilgrims kept looking around. They held their guns ready to shoot.

But instead of anything dangerous, the first thing they saw was wonderful. Fresh food!

Big clumps of fat mussels were clinging to the rocks.

*The Pilgrims searched
the coast for a
place to settle.*

The Pilgrims pried them open with their knives and gobbled up the sweet, soft flesh. Even raw, they were delicious. The men ate and ate.

Finally they waded back out to the rowboat and returned to the *Mayflower*. The Pilgrims still needed the ship to sleep in at night while they planned and built their settlement. And they were grateful to the captain, Master Christopher Jones, for not sailing back to England right away.

But after enjoying themselves on shore, the men hated going back to the damp, crowded, smelly little ship. Especially when some of them began vomiting. The mussels that they had eaten made them sick.

It was back to rock-hard biscuits and salt beef.

☼

The next day the Pilgrims went exploring again. They drank fresh water from a stream.

And they found an Indian corn field. At one side was a heap of sand. Digging there, the Pilgrims made an interesting and valuable discovery: baskets of dried, many-colored Indian corn.

The kernels would make good seeds, so the Pilgrims kept them to plant in the spring.

But now they had to hurry and build their houses. It was already November and getting very cold. Pilgrim scouts looked all over.

Finally they chose a place that seemed perfect. It

was high on a hill, easy to defend if the Indians attacked. There was a good boat harbor nearby. Sweet, fresh water bubbled out of several springs, and a brook ran down the hillside. Grapevines, herbs, watercress, leeks, onions, and berries grew wild.

So did flax and hemp, which could be used for making rope. And nearby was good clay for making pots.

Plenty of fish lived in the ocean—cod, turbot, herring. There were also lobsters, crabs, and mussels (if the Pilgrims dared to eat them).

There were even whales. The Pilgrims had seen them swimming and playing near the *Mayflower*. Whales would provide meat, oil, and ivory.

Birch, oak, pine, beech, and walnut trees grew close by. The Pilgrims could cut down trees and begin building their houses right away. The trees would even provide food—walnuts for the settlers and acorns for their pigs.

Best of all, some of the land had already been cleared by the Indians and was ready for planting. The settlers wouldn't have to waste time burning or chopping the thick forest. They would be able to plant their seeds as soon as spring came.

They looked around at the little field, the tall forest

*Harpooning whales
was dangerous!*

trees, the running brook, the distant ocean, and agreed: this would be their home.

And to remind themselves of their old home, they named the new town after the English town from which the *Mayflower* had sailed: Plymouth.

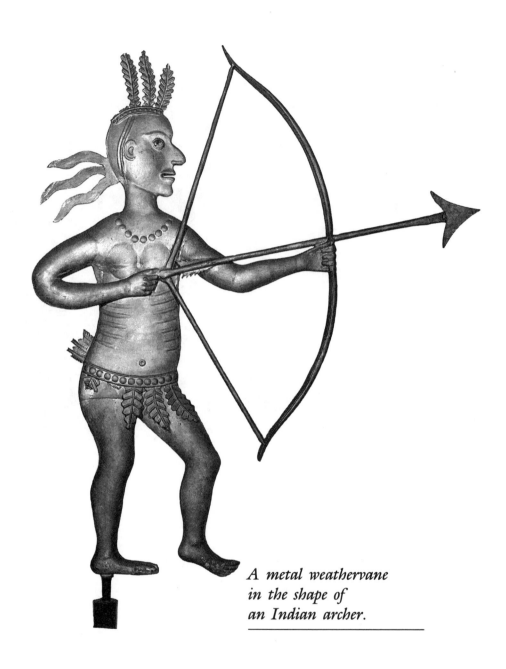

*A metal weathervane
in the shape of
an Indian archer.*

# 3

# Eating on the Run

❂

The right time to dine—for
a rich man, when he is hungry;
for a poor man, when he has
something to eat.

—Velez de Guevara,
*Sobremesa*

*T*he Pilgrims planned
their new town carefully. A street would run up the
hillside with houses and gardens on each side. At the
top, there would be a wooden gun platform for pro-
tection.

The crew of the *Mayflower* helped the Pilgrims drag
six cannons up from the ship. It was hard work. The

largest of the guns was ten feet long and weighed almost a ton. Even the ammunition was heavy. The cannons fired big iron balls.

The Pilgrims mounted the guns on their gun platform and pointed them in different directions. Now they hoped they would be able to defend themselves against the Indians.

They were becoming more and more afraid of an Indian attack. They knew they would find it hard to defend themselves. Some of the Pilgrims had died, and many who survived were sick and weak. Among the dead was the governor, John Carver. William Bradford was chosen to be the new governor of Plymouth.

Whenever a person died, his friends buried him or her secretly, at night. This way, if the Indians were spying on them, they wouldn't know how few of the Pilgrims were left.

One of the Pilgrims, Miles Standish, had another idea to fool the Indians. He told all the healthy men to march up and down with their rifles. Sometimes they fired into the air. Standish hoped the Indians would think the Pilgrims had a big army, and would be afraid to attack.

SANCTORUM MEMORIA SIT BEATA

HERE LYETH BURIED
Ye BODY OF
MR TIMOTHY LINDALL
AGED 56 YEARS
& 7 MO. DECEASED
JANUARY Ye 6
1 6 9 8/9

*After the first
year, the Pilgrims
carved tombstones.*

And then, one day, an Indian walked into their settlement!

The frightened Pilgrims ran for their guns.

Indians looked different. They wore hardly any clothing, and the Pilgrims wore as much as possible.

Indians decorated themselves with beads, seashells, paint, and bear grease. The Pilgrims thought decorating yourself was sinful.

And of course the Pilgrims couldn't understand the Indian's language.

But this Indian spoke English! Before the Pilgrims could shoot, he said in a loud voice, "Hello, Englishmen!" The Englishmen were astonished.

His name was Samoset. He acted like a friend. But was he one?

The Pilgrims gave Samoset some food to eat. They gave him a place to sleep. They watched him carefully.

The next day he returned to the forest. But soon he

came again, and this time he brought with him another Indian named Squanto.

Squanto had actually been to England. In fact, he had been there twice! Early English explorers had brought him. He could speak English well.

Squanto and Samoset introduced the Pilgrims to Massasoit, the chief of the Indians who lived nearby.

Massasoit came to the meeting with some of his braves. The braves' faces were painted black. But Chief Massasoit's face was painted dark red. Around his neck he wore a chain of white bone beads. A knife hung from the chain.

The Pilgrims gave Massasoit cushions to sit on and many presents. They told him that King James of England wished to be his friend.

Massasoit agreed to become friends with the English. He made a treaty with the Pilgrim leaders. It said that the Pilgrims and the Indians would not fight each other.

This was a good agreement. It worked. The Pilgrims didn't have to spend time fighting. They could build, hunt, and grow their crops.

Squanto, the Indian who had been to England, helped the Pilgrims so much that they believed God must have sent him to them.

He helped them make the agreement with Chief Massasoit. And he taught them something very, very important—the Indian way to plant corn.

✺

Indian corn helped keep the Pilgrims alive. After they got off the *Mayflower,* food was harder to find than they had expected. Was America really a land of plenty?

Their ship's supplies were running low. The beer that they loved to drink was all gone. Now they had to choke down the hard ship's biscuits with only water.

The people who were sick needed nourishing food. The captain of the *Mayflower* shot some geese for them to eat. He shot some seals, too. Seals were not a regular food. But the Pilgrims were hungry enough to eat almost anything.

They had to work all the time, taking care of sick people, building houses, and trying to find enough to eat. They hunted and fished but couldn't catch much. They were always hungry and always tired.

Families hardly ever sat down to a meal together. With all their work, there wasn't enough time. They

ate whatever they could find—a handful of berries or nuts, some leftover biscuits, a few dried peas. They had barely enough food to keep them alive.

There was no ceremony and little politeness. People just grabbed whatever they could and ate it on the run as they dashed off to split logs or look for more food.

Things were just as hard for the crew of the *Mayflower*. Their ship was supposed to sail back to England. But many of the sailors grew sick, and half of them died. So the captain decided to stay in Plymouth until the winter was over.

He knew that his small crew of sick men would not be able to sail the *Mayflower* through stormy winter seas.

✺

By the time the *Mayflower* finally sailed back to England, on April 5, 1621, the Pilgrims had built several small houses and planted crops.

The following autumn, they gathered their first harvest. Their English grains had not done well. But there was a fine supply of Indian corn! Governor William Bradford decided to hold a celebration—a day of thanksgiving.

The first year in America had been so hard that only four Pilgrim women were still alive. They needed help preparing the feast.

The children went to the stream and the seashore to gather eels, clams, mussels, and oysters. They found wild onions, leeks, and watercress to make a **sallet** (salad).

Governor Bradford sent four men out to shoot wild birds, and they returned with ducks, geese, and turkeys. To complete the meal there were dried plums and berries, corn-flour bread, and grape wine.

Then company arrived! The Indian chief Massasoit came. The Pilgrims had invited him. But they had not expected him to arrive with ninety braves!

The Pilgrims were worried. They didn't have enough food to feed so many people. They needed to save some of their food for the coming winter.

But Massasoit understood. He sent his best hunters into the woods. The braves brought back five deer and gave them to the Pilgrims.

Now there was enough food for everyone. The first Thanksgiving was a wonderful celebration.

The Pilgrims had done many important things in their first year. They had started a town. They had made friends with the Indians. And they had begun to grow corn, the crop that would keep them alive.

They looked forward to the future with hope and courage.

*Roofs were made of coarse
grass or cattails.*

# 4

# Welcome!

Come in the evening,
or come in the morning,
Come when you're looked for,
or come without warning.

—Thomas O. Davis,
*The Welcome*

*W*hat sort of houses did the Pilgrims live in?

When they first came ashore from the *Mayflower*, they were cold. They were hungry. They were tired. They were worried about Indians and afraid of wild animals.

They needed shelter right away. There wasn't time

for separate houses. So everyone pitched in to help build a community house. It had only one big, square room. The Pilgrims crowded into it. There wasn't any furniture—not even a floor. They slept right on the ground.

But then there was a serious accident. A fire, started by a spark from cooking, destroyed the community house. The weary Pilgrims had to build another one.

Little by little, families built their own houses. They made them out of wood, with stone fireplaces. At first, each house had only one room. It was called the **hall**.

Everything happened in the hall. Were you hungry? You ate in the hall, right in front of the fireplace where the food was cooked.

Did you want to play inside? Or work quietly by the warm fire, mending shoes, whittling tools, or making brooms? You sat in the hall. There wasn't anywhere else!

At night you went to bed right there in the same room. When you woke up, you helped push the beds back against the walls so people would have space to walk around. It was a crowded way to live.

The floor was the earth itself. The ceiling was so low that a tall person's head could easily bump up

*This cradle kept
a Pilgrim baby
warm and snug.*

against it. Even children could bump into the clumps of vegetables and fruits, strung on grapevines, that had been hung from the ceiling to dry.

The door was made of wooden planks nailed together. For privacy and safety, every door had a latch on the inside. A string was tied to the latch, and the other end of the string was poked outside through a little hole in the door.

To open the door from outside, you pulled a peg, called a **latchkey**, to lift the latch. Before going to bed, the people inside would pull in the latch string. Then no one could come in while they were sleeping.

✷

The Pilgrims went to sleep soon after dark and were up at daylight. But even during the day, the hall was dark. It had only one or two windows. They were small, to keep the cold air out, and were covered with oiled paper or thin sheets of animal horn. Only a little light came through.

Later, the Pilgrims sent for glass from England. Glass helped keep out the cold. But glass windows were so expensive that windows stayed small.

More light was needed. Of course, electric lights hadn't been invented yet. Pilgrim women made **rush-lights**. A rush is a kind of thick grass with a hollow stem.

One end of the rush was dipped into bear grease or moose fat. The other end was stuck between the bricks of the fireplace. Then the greasy end was set on fire. Rushlights gave only a little light, but they were quick and easy to make.

Bear grease and moose fat were also used to make candles. Later, when the Pilgrims had more time to spare, they made candles from bayberries. Bayberry candles were a big improvement. They took longer to make, but they smelled much better than animal-fat candles.

**Betty lamps**, too, gave light. Betty lamps were little metal dishes with handles and spouts. They burned fish oil. A linen wick was stuck into the spout and set on fire. The fish oil burned slowly, lasted a long time, and smelled awful.

✹

The dark, smoky hall always smelled of animal fat, fish oil, and people. The Pilgrims didn't like to take baths. They thought soap and water were bad for you.

But in addition to the awful smells, there were the nice smells of herbs and flowers. Bundles of dried parsley, sage, marjoram, rosemary, and marigolds hung from the rafters.

Smoke from the fireplace helped to keep the herbs dry. When the cook needed an herb for the soup, she just reached up, broke off some dried leaves, and crumbled them into the pot.

If she wanted to make the house smell even nicer, a Pilgrim woman sprinkled bits of herbs among the rushes underfoot. Before their houses had floors, the Pilgrims used thick layers of rushes to keep out the chill of the earth.

Even so, houses were very, very cold in winter.

Most of the heat from the fireplace went up the chimney—even though smoke from the fire came into the room. If you sat right in front of the blazing fire, your face might burn but your back would freeze.

So the Pilgrims built special benches called **settles**. They had high backs and sides. Settles were placed in front of the fire. Their high backs kept cold drafts away.

They also built other furniture—stools, chairs, and tables. The first tables were made from wooden packing boxes that the Pilgrims had brought on the *Mayflower*.

And at least two beds were crowded into the hall. A four-poster bed for the parents had a cloth roof draped on top. Curtains hung down the sides. It was like a little room. The roof and curtains made it private and slightly warmer.

Under the big bed was a low one, called a **trundle bed**. At night, the trundle bed was pulled out. The children—usually many of them—would squeeze into it. They helped keep each other warm.

Beds weren't very comfortable. Mattresses were stuffed with straw, corn husks, oak leaves, or cattails. They were lumpy and scratchy.

And the Pilgrims' beds were short. Adults slept half sitting up on big pillows. If they tried to stretch out, their feet hung over the end—and froze.

In winter, the Pilgrims' feet were *always* cold. These first settlers didn't wear socks or stockings. Their pants had straps at the bottom to slip their feet through, so the pants legs wouldn't ride up. The Pilgrims put their shoes right on over the straps.

At night, they would put a **warming pan** in the icy bed. This was a covered copper pan filled with hot embers from the fire. The pan was moved back and forth under the sheets to warm them up before the shivering Pilgrims crawled in to go to sleep.

When they got out of bed in the morning, they pushed the children's trundle bed back under the parents' four-poster bed to make more space in the crowded hall.

The Pilgrims had very large families. Sometimes

*Mrs. Elizabeth Lott . . .*

*. . . and Mr. George Lott*

there wasn't enough room in the trundle bed for all the children. Then some of them slept on the table! After dinner was cleared and the crumbs brushed away, they climbed right up and went to sleep. In the morning, they awoke, yawned, climbed off the table, and were ready for breakfast.

✿

The Pilgrims who came on the *Mayflower* were happy with their crude little houses. Smoke, darkness, and crowding didn't bother them. Their homes in England hadn't been much more comfortable.

But Pilgrim life slowly changed. Every year, more shiploads of people arrived. The settlement at Plymouth grew, and new settlements were begun.

Everyone still worked hard. They grew crops, caught fish, trapped animals, and traded with the Indians for furs that they sent back to England. Soon the Pilgrims who had come on the *Mayflower* were able to pay back the money they owed to the Merchant Adventurers.

Then they started to improve their houses. They added rooms upstairs for sleeping and for storing food. Sometimes children shared their bedrooms with barrels of apples and sacks of beans and peas.

Most people also dug little storage rooms *under* their houses. These were called **root cellars**. Root vegetables—carrots, sweet potatoes, turnips, and Jerusalem artichokes—were piled in the cool, dark cellars. So were barrels of pickled or salted food.

The Pilgrim period of American history lasted from 1620, when the *Mayflower* sailed, until 1691, when Plymouth Colony became part of the Massachusetts Bay Colony. It was a time of great changes. Hardships eased and life improved.

Craftsmen came, bringing much-needed skills. Among them were **sawyers** (workers who saw lumber into planks), **tanners** (who cure animal skins), **coopers** (barrel makers), and expert furniture makers.

Even artists came. They painted pictures of some of the Pilgrims. We can still look at a portrait of Edward

*Edward Winslow,*
*a Pilgrim leader.*

Winslow, the Pilgrim who agreed to be a hostage for Chief Massasoit while the Pilgrims and the Indians were working out their treaty.

The new settlers brought more pigs, sheep, and goats. They brought cows for milk and beef, and horses for farm work. They brought seeds and farming tools. Food became more plentiful.

As the years went by, the Pilgrims sent back to England for furniture, rugs, linens, and dishes of silver and **pewter**—a metal made by melting tin with lead or copper. Their comfortable homes became very different from the dark, cold little huts that had been their first shelter in America.

*The big fireplace was
used for cooking in
a Pilgrim house.*

# 5

# The Heart of
# the House

✹

We may live without poetry,
        music and art;
We may live without conscience,
        and live without heart;
We may live without friends,
        we may live without books;
But civilized man
        may not live without cooks.

—Owen Meredith (E. R.
Bulwer-Lytton), *Lucile*

*C*ooking was the most important activity in a Pilgrim household. It went on for hour after hour—sometimes all day. It took the Pilgrims much longer to prepare food than it takes us.

They cooked in a stone fireplace eight or ten feet wide. It took up a whole wall. The huge logs that burned in it were sometimes dragged right into the room by horses!

The fire was the heart of the house. No one took fire for granted. It was hard to make a fire. Once you had one, it was best to keep it going.

But a blazing fire was dangerous. A little wooden house could be burned up in a few minutes.

So before the family went to bed, someone always raked ashes carefully over the hot embers. Ashes made the fire burn more slowly and kept some sparks glowing.

In the morning, the cook fanned the sparks. They burst into flames. Fresh logs were piled on. Soon the room sparkled again with heat and light.

The day's cooking could begin.

❂

A thick bar, called a **lug pole**, stretched across the fireplace, directly above the fire. Pots and kettles hung from it. The lug pole was made of green wood so it wouldn't dry out and burn up.

If it ever did catch fire, all the pots and kettles crashed into the fireplace. The food was ruined. Sometimes the cook got burned or even killed. So the Pilgrims replaced their old lug poles with fresh green ones often.

After a few years, some of the settlers began to make iron hardware. It was much safer to have fire-proof iron lug poles, and iron hooks to hang pots from. Iron chains raised and lowered the food to control the cooking temperature.

One pot hanging from the lug pole was always filled with hot water. Others held the soups and stews that were the Pilgrims' main meals.

Usually there was a pot for puddings, which the Pilgrims called **spoon meats**. They used the word *meat* to mean any kind of food. Spoon meat was food you ate with a spoon.

In England, their favorite spoon meat had been **hasty pudding**. They made it by boiling water and wheat flour in a cloth bag. As the pudding cooked, the wheat flour absorbed the water. It swelled and filled the bag.

But in America, where they had trouble growing wheat, they made their old favorite with corn flour. They called it Indian pudding, because the Indians had taught them how to cook with corn.

*Pudding*

Indian pudding had to boil for hours. The Pilgrims ate so much of it that a heavy pot of Indian pudding was kept steaming and bubbling over the fire almost all the time.

Not all pots hung from the lug pole. The Pilgrims also used three-legged pots, pans, and kettles that stood right in the fire. Hot embers were shoveled onto their lids. The tremendous heat cooked the food inside quickly.

✦

Most of the meat the Pilgrims ate was salted or pickled and then stewed. Roast meat was a rare and special treat for them. When someone shot or trapped a bear or a moose, everybody feasted.

A sharp iron rod with a pointed end, called a **spit**, was stuck all the way through the meat. The two ends of the spit rested on iron legs, called **andirons**. The spit had a handle attached. Someone—usually a

child—was given the job of turning the spit so the meat would cook on all sides.

If the family didn't own a spit, the cook attached the meat to a rope. She tied the other end of the rope over a hook in the ceiling, right in front of the fireplace.

Then she twirled the meat to twist the rope as hard and tight as she could. It slowly untwisted, twisted up the other way, and untwisted again, turning around and around in front of the fire. When it stopped, she wound it up again. In this way the meat was gradually roasted on all sides.

✪

Breads were baked in many ways.

Sometimes small loaves of bread were wrapped in clean leaves and then laid in the hot ashes.

Corn bread and biscuits were often baked in a covered, three-legged iron pot called a **bake kettle**.

Little round breads called **hoecakes** were baked on the edge of a hoe, which was stuck into the hot ashes at the edge of the fire.

**Johnnycakes**—little round cakes of cornmeal and water—were baked on a board that was propped in front of the fire. Johnnycakes cooked quickly and were served at almost every meal.

Travelers found johnnycakes easy to carry in their pockets. In fact, some people think they were invented for taking on trips and were originally called "journey cakes."

The Pilgrims did their best to make an English-style bread. They mixed ground Indian corn with a little of their precious rye flour. They called this bread **rye 'n Injun**. It was a Pilgrim favorite.

When they didn't have corn flour, the Pilgrims made bread with bean flour. Bean-flour bread was called **horsebread**. It tasted so awful that the Pilgrims sometimes fed it to their pigs.

❂

Most fireplaces had a special bake oven built right into the chimney.

Once a week, a big fire was built in the bake oven. While it was burning, the cook mixed bread dough and formed it into loaves. She placed the loaves on a flat wooden shovel called a **bread peel**.

When the oven was hot enough, she raked out the wood and ashes. Then she spread oak leaves on the floor of the hot oven. The leaves were gathered by children every fall and stored on pointed sticks next to the fireplace.

The cook slid the bread peel into the oven. She twisted it quickly. The loaves of bread slid off onto the leaves. She pulled out the bread peel and sealed up the oven.

The bread was left to cook all night. In the morning the oven was opened and the crusty, brown loaves were taken out and piled on the table, smelling wonderful. The family ate their first meal of the day in the warm, smoky light of the huge fireplace.

*Pilgrim men carried
their muskets everywhere.
They were afraid of
Indian attacks.*

# 6

# We All Scream
# for Pudding

Tell me what you eat
and I'll tell you what you are.

—Anthelme Brillat Savarin,
*Physiologie du Goût*

*T*he Pilgrims did not turn into Americans the minute they stepped off the *Mayflower* in 1620.

They still thought of themselves as English. And they still wanted the English food that they were used to—meat, bread, and pudding, all washed down with plenty of beer.

So when the snows of their first American winter had melted away, and the days grew longer with the coming of spring, they went to work with their hoes and shovels, breaking up the hard earth. Then they planted the precious wheat, barley, and rye seeds that they had brought from home.

Everyone watched the growing plants anxiously. If there was a fine harvest in the fall, they would be able to cook the wheat puddings and pies that had been their favorite foods back in England.

But the Pilgrims were disappointed. Hardly any wheat came up, and only a little barley and rye.

The crop that flourished was Indian corn. The corn seeds that the Pilgrims had found the first day they came ashore probably saved their lives.

So, instead of wheat or barley, the settlers made their bread with ground corn. They didn't think it tasted as good as wheat bread, but they were happy to have it. Corn kept them from starving.

❂

Bread was very important, but it wasn't enough. English people also wanted meat. They loved it roasted or baked in pie crusts. To the Pilgrims, a pie was not a dessert. It was a delicious way of cooking meat and bread together.

At first, finding any meat to eat was a problem. The salted meat that had been left over from the *Mayflower* voyage was quickly eaten.

And it turned out to be hard to shoot wild animals. The Pilgrims' guns made a tremendous noise and weren't very accurate. If a hunter shot and missed, all the animals ran away.

The Pilgrims weren't good at trapping, either. They saw many animals in the woods, but were rarely able to catch them.

Sometimes the Indians traded deer meat to the Pilgrims in exchange for beads and knives. The Pilgrims were delighted. Back in England, only the richest people ever ate deer meat.

The Indians were excellent trappers. Once, when William Bradford went to look at an unusual tree, it turned out to be an Indian trap! He was jerked up into the air and hung by one foot until his friends cut him down.

✿

English people didn't like fruit. But the Pilgrims planted apple, pear, and peach seedlings as soon as they could. They wanted to make **cider** from the fruit.

Apples were made into apple cider. **Perry** cider was made from pears. **Peachy** cider came from peaches.

Families kept their cider in barrels called **hogsheads**. Everyone drank cider all year long.

Though the Pilgrims preferred to drink their fruit, hunger forced them to eat it, too. In the spring, the children were sent to search for wild plums and berries. Sometimes people had to eat any food that would keep them alive.

The Pilgrims didn't like vegetables, either. They didn't consider them real food. In England, they had used them mostly as seasonings or decorations. But when they arrived in America, sometimes the choice was a vegetarian meal or no meal at all.

They called vegetables **herbs** and **roots**. Herbs were leafy vegetables that grew aboveground and could be made into salads. Roots—like potatoes and carrots—grew underground. The Pilgrims cooked roots in stews, or put them in the ashes of the fire to bake.

If they had to eat vegetables, they made them as tasty as possible. The Pilgrims loved spicy food. Back home in England, people sometimes used five or six spices to flavor one dish. Pepper, mace, cloves, cinnamon, cardamon, and ginger were their favorites. And to give their food an interesting color, they liked to add beet juice, spinach juice, or dried marigold petals.

During the first hungry years, the Pilgrims didn't have many of these ingredients. The spices they had brought with them on the *Mayflower* were soon used up. They usually ate simple food because that was all they had. But they never stopped longing for the colorful, spicy, starchy food they had known and loved back in England.

*Muskets were loud
and unreliable. Often
Pilgrim hunters missed
their targets, scaring
the game away.*

# 7

# What's Cooking?

❀

Davy, Davy Dumpling
  Boil him in the pot;
Sugar him and butter him,
  And eat him while he's hot.

—nursery rhyme

*F*ood, food, food!

It was hard for the first Pilgrim settlers to think about anything else.

America *looked* like an easy place to find food. The sky was full of birds. Sometimes thousands of geese flew over—so many that they blocked out the sun and the day grew dark.

There were many animals to hunt. Deer, moose, elk, and bears lived in the forest. The ocean and streams were full of fish.

But the Pilgrims hadn't brought fish hooks of the right size on the *Mayflower*. And they weren't good at hunting or trapping. They ate the last of their ship's supplies and searched for wild vegetables and fruit. They were hungry almost all the time.

✺

The Pilgrims might have starved to death if Squanto hadn't taught them how to plant Indian corn.

He showed them how to heap up little mounds of earth. In each mound they buried five corn seeds and five herrings. As the herring rotted, it became a wonderful fertilizer. The corn plants came up green and healthy.

But the herring caused a problem, too. Its smell at-tracted wolves. They came to the corn fields to dig up the herring and eat it.

This would ruin the corn, so children stood guard in the fields. They kept a pile of stones to throw at the wolves. It was scary work.

When the corn was ready, everybody helped to har-vest it. Some corn was roasted and eaten right on the cob.

More often, the kernels had to be taken off the cobs. Children scraped the kernels off with the sharp edge of a shovel.

Sometimes the corn kernels were boiled together with wood ashes. The ashes and water made lye. A strong solution of lye made the husks of the kernels fall off.

Then the Pilgrims cooked the soft insides of the kernels to make a cereal called **hominy**. Or else they added them to soups and stews.

But most of the corn kernels were pounded into flour. Pounding corn was hard work. The Indians showed the Pilgrims a trick that made the work much easier.

To pound corn the Indian way, you tied the pounding stone to the top of a young tree, so that it hung clear of the ground. When you pulled the pounding stone down, the tree bent. You made the pounding stone smash against another flat stone, which was covered with corn.

Then, when you let go, the tree and the stone shot back up into the air. That way, you didn't have to lift it over and over again. Slowly, one smash at a time, the corn was ground into flour.

❂

Corn flour was baked into breads and puddings that people ate at every meal. There wasn't much variety in the diet of the first Pilgrims.

For breakfast they had pudding, bread, and a cup of beer.

The midday meal, which they called dinner, was their biggest of the day. In the early years, it was just like breakfast—beer, pudding, and bread. The only difference was that the portions were larger. In later years, when they had the ingredients, cooks chopped up vegetables and meat to make soups and stews.

The last meal of the day was supper. Once again, the same dishes appeared—pudding, leftover bread, and, of course, beer.

And after supper was finished, the cook mixed ground corn and water in a big kettle and hung it over the embers to cook all night. In the morning, breakfast would be ready to eat. Pudding again!

❂

Slowly the Pilgrims prospered. They had more food to eat. And they had more *kinds* of foods—especially meat.

They had brought a few pigs with them on the *Mayflower*. The pigs loved America. Instead of fencing the pigs in, people fenced in their gardens and crops. The pigs got to run around and eat anything they could find.

So within a few years the Pilgrims had plenty of pig meat. They roasted and ate some of it. Some they preserved and stored away to eat later. They traded some to the Indians, too. The Indians didn't have pigs, but they thought pork was delicious. They gave the Pilgrims deer meat in exchange for pork.

Some people were able to trap rabbits, which they roasted or stewed. And sometimes a lucky Pilgrim hunter shot a bear or a moose.

Every family had chickens but rarely got to eat them, because eggs were so important. The chickens laid their eggs in the little Pilgrim gardens, where they scratched around continually in search of food. Every day, children would hunt through the garden to find fresh eggs.

*A bear could provide
a family with meat
for many days.*

Eggs were roasted, boiled, fried, or baked in custards called **white pots**. Extra eggs were pickled in vinegar or buried in baskets of fat and straw. These methods of preserving kept them good to eat for a long time.

❀

Four years after the first Pilgrims arrived, some new settlers brought a bull and a cow to Plymouth. They became the parents of a large herd, which provided beef and milk.

The milk was welcome, especially for the children. **Pap**—a mixture of milk and flour—was the first food Pilgrim babies ate. Their next food was meat. A Pilgrim mother would cut meat into tiny bits. Then she would chew it herself to make it soft enough for her little baby to swallow.

*Milk was used in cooking.*

But as soon as a child was old enough to hold a cup, he or she was given beer to drink. The Pilgrims didn't like drinking plain milk. Instead they used it in puddings and cakes and made it into butter and cheese. The leftover liquid—whey—was fed to the pigs.

*

After the first hard years, the Pilgrims were never again in danger of starving. As soon as they had enough food, they began to think about making it taste good.

That meant spices.

At first, they sent to England whenever they needed spices. But then the Pilgrims found a cheaper source. They began to trade with settlers in the West Indies, where many spices grew.

The Pilgrims sent salted fish, pickled beef, and lumber. In return, the West Indian merchants sent back cinnamon, ginger, cloves, nutmeg, and cardamon—plus molasses and sugar, which were baked into puddings and pies.

Salt was the most important spice of all. The Pilgrims had brought salt with them from England. And after that ran out, they made their own from the salty Atlantic. They filled shallow pans with seawater and let it evaporate in the sun, leaving salt on the bottom. A sprinkle of salt made even vegetables taste good!

They also used salt to preserve meat and fish. They needed preserved food for winter, when no fresh food could be found. And they used preserved food for trade with the West Indies and with England.

There is only one problem with food preserved in salt: before you can eat it, you have to rinse out most of the salt. You have to rinse it again and again and again. If you don't, it tastes terrible.

That meant someone had to run down to the near-
est stream, fill a pitcher, and carry it back to the
house. Sometimes many trips were needed. This was
hard work, especially in the middle of the icy, freezing
winter.

So Pilgrim cooks learned a trick. They cooked
salted food with bits of bread, plus a handful of corn
flour or dried peas. These ingredients absorbed some
of the salt. The stew was served with more bread, or
perhaps with a boiled pudding.

That took some of the sting out of a salty mouthful.

✸

Salt, spices, sugar, and molasses changed the Pilgrim
diet tremendously. Plain puddings and breads were

still an important part of every meal. But now most meals also included some sweet or spicy dishes.

Another major change was the Pilgrims' gradual acceptance of fruits and vegetables. In the early years, they had eaten them only out of desperation, when they couldn't find the familiar English foods that they preferred.

Now they found themselves *choosing* to eat fruits and vegetables. Perhaps to their surprise, they had come to enjoy them. This was one of the many small ways in which English settlers were slowly turning into Americans.

*A portrait of the
Mason children—David,
Joanna, and Abigail—
painted in 1670.*

# 8

# Don't Throw Your Bones on the Floor

✦

Manners in the dining room,
Manners in the hall,
If you don't behave yourself,
You shan't have none at all.

—old rhyme

The first Pilgrim settlers still thought of England as "home." Though they had come to America to worship in their own way, they weren't planning to create a new country. They still wanted to be English.

And when they told their children to be good, they meant to be like English children—like the children

✿ 73

they themselves had been, many years ago and thousands of miles across the sea.

More than twenty children sailed on the *Mayflower*. And one baby was born while the *Mayflower* was at sea. His parents named him Oceanus.

Another baby, Peregrine White, was born aboard the *Mayflower* a month after it arrived in America. "Peregrine" means "pilgrim." He lived to be seventy-eight years old.

During the first hard winter in Plymouth, almost half the grown-ups died. But almost all the children survived.

✪

Pilgrim parents were strict with their children. Some of the rules sound familiar, like this one (from a book called *The School of Manners*) about speaking with your mouth full:

> When your meat is in your mouth,
> do not drink or speak or laugh—
> Dame Courtesy forbids.

But Pilgrim manners weren't always the same as ours. In their first years in America, they were often

too busy for regular meals. People just helped themselves right out of the cooking pot. They ate stand-
ing—in front of the fire, if the day was cold—and
then hurried off to work again.

When the family did eat together, the dinner table
was often just some old boards laid on top of barrels.
The cooking pot was placed in the middle, and the
family gathered around.

Later, when the Pilgrims had more time—and
more dishes—food was brought to the table on large,
round platters called **chargers**.

No one had his or her own plate. Instead, two people would share a **trencher**—a bowl carved or burned
out of a block of wood.

A mother and father shared a trencher. Children
shared, too. The Pilgrims thought that people who
had their own trenchers were show-offs.

Some poor people didn't have wooden trenchers.
Instead, they used pieces of stale bread as plates. They
put the food on top. Then, after they had eaten the
food, they ate the bread plates!

Almost nobody used a fork. One Pilgrim, Governor
John Winthrop, was given a fork as a present. It
had only two tines. The Pilgrims called it a "double
dagger."

They thought forks were silly. Why bother, they said. "Fingers were made before forks."

But everyone needed a spoon, because the Pilgrims ate so many soups and stews. The first spoons made in Plymouth were clamshells attached to sticks.

Buffalo horns made good spoons, too. You scooped up the food with the open end. Later, when they had more time, people carved spoons out of wood. Some lucky folks had brought pewter or silver spoons from England.

And everyone had his or her own knife. If you were a grown-up, it was okay to stick your knife right into the pot and pull out a piece of food. But children

*Clamshells were used to make spoons.*

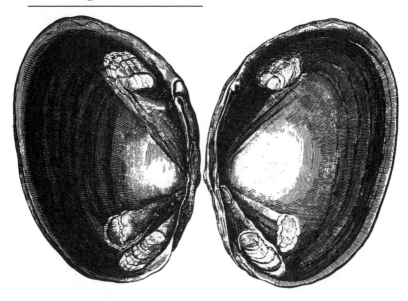

weren't supposed to take any food for themselves. They were supposed to eat whatever their parents handed to them.

It was always fine to eat with your fingers. The only rule was that you were supposed to wash them—or at least wipe them—before you stuck them in the pot.

Naturally, this meant that everyone needed a napkin. A big napkin! The Pilgrims threw it over one shoulder or tied it around their necks. It hung down almost to their knees. And your napkin wasn't just for wiping your hands. You could use it to grab pieces of hot food.

Often, a Pilgrim family had only one chair, and the father was the one who sat in it. The other family members sat on stools, sections of tree trunk, or wooden benches without backs.

Children sometimes had to stand at the table. In some families, this was because there was nothing for them to sit on. Other families made children stand just because they thought it was good manners. They thought it was rude for a child to sit down when a grown-up was in the room.

Sometimes children had to stand at a separate little table. They came to the main table to have their trenchers filled.

An English book of manners called *The Little Children's Little Book* gave these rules:

> Put not thy fingers in the dish,
> Neither in flesh, neither in fish.
> Put not thy meat into the salt,
> Into the cellar, that is a fault;
> But lay it fairly thee before,
> Upon thy trencher, that is good lore.

Men and boys were allowed to keep their hats on while they were eating. They needed to take them off only to drink a toast.

A polite person did not scratch at the table. Most people had lice and fleas living in their hair and clothes. But it was good manners to wait until you were done eating to scratch. It wasn't pleasant to see your neighbor mash a flea and then reach into the trencher you were sharing.

A big bowl of salt was placed in the center of the table. Important guests sat near the father, toward the head of the table—"above the salt." Children and other less important people were near the foot of the table—"below the salt."

It was very bad manners to dip your food right into

*A portrait of
Mrs. Elizabeth Feake
and her baby, Mary.*

the salt bowl. The salt would get sticky. You were supposed to take salt only with a clean knife.

If you wanted bread, you broke a piece off the loaf with your hands. You could use it to mop up your plate.

When you were eating meat, what did you do with the bones? Throwing them on the ground was considered poor manners. And you weren't supposed to put them back in the pot. The correct thing was to pile them neatly on the table.

✪

When they ran out of beer, the Pilgrims had to drink water. So they kept a bucket of drinking water on the table.

They had different kinds of cups. Some were made out of gourds, which grew on vines. The Pilgrims picked the gourds, scooped out the seeds, and dried them in the sun.

Other cups, called **noggins**, were carved from wood. A noggin had eight sides and a handle.

A cup with a hinged top was called a **tankard**. You flipped up the top to drink. Tankards were made out of wood, clay, or pewter.

The Pilgrims had even brought from England special cups made out of boiled leather and waterproofed with tar. These were called **blackjacks**. People from other countries who had seen the English drinking from leather cups were astonished. They said that Englishmen drank out of their boots!

But most Pilgrim families owned only one or two cups. During a meal, they dipped them in the beer barrel or the water bucket and passed them around the table. Everyone took a drink before passing the cup on to the next person.

The Pilgrims didn't know they were passing germs with their cups. They were living the same way their parents and their grandparents had always lived. And it wasn't just because they were poor.

They didn't *want* a lot of cups and dishes. They thought it was better to live simply. They didn't want to seem like show-offs.

And they were used to sharing. It seemed right to them. It was good manners.

*Pilgrim children
usually stood at
the table. Often they
shared a plate.*

# 9

# Eating the Plates

✦

Wilful waste brings woeful want
And you may live to say,
How I wish I had that crust
That once I threw away.

—Thomas Fuller,
*Gnomologia*

*I*t wasn't hard to clean up after a Pilgrim meal.

Especially if you ate the plates.

Even stale-bread plates usually tasted okay when hot food had soaked into them. And if they were *really* stale—as hard as rocks—the pigs were always happy to eat them.

Wooden trenchers weren't much of a cleaning problem, either. There was nothing left on them. Finishing your food was good manners. You ate every bit of it, then mopped your trencher with a piece of bread. And when you were done, you wiped your trencher with your napkin.

At the end of the meal, a big basket—called a **voider**—was passed around the table. All the trenchers and spoons were put into it. The cups and platters were put in, too, and taken away to be cleaned.

Then the men and boys lifted the table boards off their bases and leaned them against the wall. Room had to be made for other kinds of work.

The women and girls wiped the cups, spoons, and trenchers and put them away on a shelf. They didn't wash them because they didn't have running water. If any pewter tableware had been used, it was scoured with horsetail rushes. These were stalks of a coarse grass that grew in swamps.

Nobody minded if the dishes weren't perfectly clean. People did the best they could. The Pilgrims weren't fussy. They were grateful just to have food to put on their plates.

If the heavy cooking pot got burned and dirty, the

*A small Pilgrim cooking pot.*

women dragged it down to the stream. They kneeled at the edge of the water and rubbed sand or gravel inside the pot to get off the burned food. Then they rinsed the pot in the clear, cold stream.

❉

After meals, turkey wings or brooms of split birch wood were used to sweep the hearth. Ashes were swept out of the bake oven.

The dirty napkins and tablecloth were folded and put away. They were used many times between washings.

The Pilgrims washed their linens and clothes only once or twice a year. It was a tough job. Just making the soap took hours. Women made it from ashes and animal grease.

When washday came at last, a fire was lit outside the kitchen door. The men pounded two forked sticks into the ground, one on each side of the fire. They laid a thick, strong pole across the forks and hung a huge pot directly above the fire.

Then someone would have to take a bucket to the stream, fill it, and carry it back. Two children might work together, carrying a bucket between them. Water is heavy! It took several buckets of water, and several trips to the stream, to fill the pot.

At last the water began to boil and was poured into a washtub. The women rubbed soap into the dirty wash. Then they stirred it around and around in the washtub with a stick.

When the wash was clean, it was spread on bushes to dry. Pilgrims liked to do their wash in March or April, because there was plenty of sun and wind for drying.

They folded the clean, dry clothes and linens, sprinkled them with fragrant herbs and flowers, and put them in wooden boxes. But they didn't stay clean for long!

Soon it was time to eat again. Everyone got to

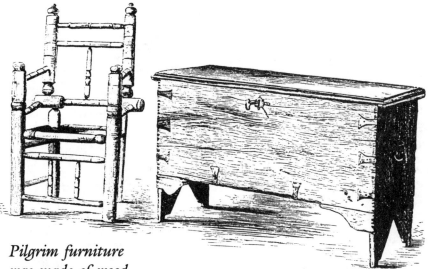

*Pilgrim furniture
was made of wood.
Instead of nails, pegs
of wood were used.*

work—opening the table, spreading the clean table-cloth, putting out the trenchers, spoons, and napkins.

The Indian pudding was given a final stir and brought to the table, steaming and sweet-smelling. Everyone grabbed a napkin and spoon and got ready to eat.

*A portrait of Anne Pollard.*

# 1 0

# Help Yourself: A Pilgrim Menu from Soup to Nuts

❂

Some hae meat and canna eat,
    And some would eat that want it;
But we hae meat and we can eat,
    And sae the Lord be thankit.

—Robert Burns,
"The Selkirk Grace"

*T*he first Pilgrims came to Plymouth more than a hundred and fifty years before the United States became an independent country—a very long time ago.

No one alive today knew a Pilgrim. Parts of their lives remain a mystery to us. We can only guess.

But we have learned many things about them by

reading their letters and diaries and looking at the pictures they drew. And there is one part of their experience that we can share: *we can eat the foods the Pilgrims ate*.

Here are ten recipes for Pilgrim food and drink. The Pilgrims, of course, did their cooking over an open fire. These recipes tell you how to prepare Pilgrim food in a modern kitchen.

You can put together a complete Pilgrim dinner, if you like. Everything is here—soup, side dishes, bread, stew, a drink, and dessert.

Or the dishes can be cooked separately. Try serving spicy cucumber catsup with hamburgers. Or bearberry jelly on toast. Swizzle is an unusual drink for a hot summer day.

Cook with an adult helper. Ask the adult to pour and carry hot foods, and to help you use sharp tools for cutting and slicing.

# A Pilgrim Menu

---

*Fresh Corn Soup*

*Red Pickled Eggs*

*Hot Indian Pudding*

*Succotash Stew*

*Spicy Cucumber Catsup*

*Bannock Cakes*

*Whole Baked Pumpkin Stuffed with Apples*

*Bearberry Jelly*

*Swizzle*

*Hot Nuts*

---

## Fresh Corn Soup

✪

Sup not Broth at Table,
but eat it with a Spoon.

—from *The School of
Manners*

Pilgrim children helped to plant and harvest corn. And they ate it—or something made with it—at almost every meal.

## INGREDIENTS

6 ears fresh corn
1½ cups water
½ cup milk
3 tablespoons butter
3 tablespoons flour
½ teaspoon salt

½ teaspoon black pepper
¼ teaspoon ground nutmeg
⅛ teaspoon ground cloves
3 cups milk
1 cup popcorn (popped)

1 • Remove husks and silk from the ears of corn. Save two green husks from inside the corn. Throw away the rest of the husks and the silk. Cut off the kernels. Set them aside.

2 • Pour one and a half cups of water and half a cup of milk into a heavy two-quart pot. Bring to a boil. Add the green husks and the corn kernels. Reduce the heat, cover, and simmer until the kernels are tender (about five minutes). Drain the corn. Set aside the kernels and throw away the liquid and the husks.

3 • Melt the butter in a three-quart pot over low heat. Add the flour, salt, black pepper, nutmeg, and cloves, stirring until the mixture is smooth. Stir in three cups of milk. Add the corn kernels. Cook, stirring often, over medium heat, until the soup is hot (about ten minutes).

4 • Pour the soup into bowls. Sprinkle each bowl with popcorn and serve at once.

*Serves 6–8*

# Red Pickled Eggs

✿

Here's a riddle that was popular in the seventeenth century:

> As I was walking in a field of wheat
> I picked up something good to eat;
> Neither fish, flesh, fowl, nor bone,
> I kept it till it ran alone.

The answer is an egg.

Sometimes pickled eggs were colored with beet or spinach juice and sliced onto a dish of salad.

### INGREDIENTS

6 *eggs*

1 *small beet*

1 *cup white vinegar*

1 *teaspoon salt*

½ *teaspoon black pepper*

½ *teaspoon red pepper*

1 *cup water*

1 • Put the eggs in a heavy one-and-a-half-quart saucepan. Add enough cold water to cover the eggs. Bring the water to a boil, turn down the heat, cover, and simmer the eggs for seventeen minutes. Drain, cool, and peel the eggs.

2 • Wash the beet. Cut off the top and part of the stem, leaving one inch of stem. Set aside.

3 • Combine vinegar, salt, black pepper, red pepper, and one cup of water. Bring to a boil.

4 • Put the peeled eggs and the beet in a one-quart glass jar. Pour the boiling vinegar mixture over them. Cool. Stir gently. Cover the jar and refrigerate overnight.

5 • In the morning, the eggs will be pink. Remove the beet. The eggs will be ready to eat.

*Serves 6*

# Hot Indian Pudding

❀

## INGREDIENTS

4 cups milk

½ cup stone-ground corn meal*

1 tablespoon butter

2 eggs

½ cup molasses

½ teaspoon salt

½ teaspoon ginger

½ teaspoon cinnamon

¼ teaspoon cloves

1 • Fill the bottom of a double boiler with water. Bring to a boil.

2 • While the water is coming to a boil, pour four cups of milk into the top of the double boiler. Place it on a burner and cook the milk over medium heat until bubbles form around the edges.

3 • Stir the cornmeal into the bubbling milk. Keep stirring until the mixture is smooth. Remove it from the heat.

4 • Put the top of the double boiler over the bottom. Cook, stirring often, over medium heat, until the cornmeal mixture thickens slightly (about fifteen minutes).

* Stone-ground cornmeal is made from whole kernels of corn—the skins of the kernels as well as the soft inside parts. It is very nutritious.

5 • Preheat the oven to 300 degrees. Butter a one-and-a-half-quart baking dish.

6 • Mix together the eggs, molasses, salt, ginger, cinnamon, and cloves. Stir them into the cornmeal mixture. Pour the mixture into the buttered baking dish. Place in the oven and bake until a knife poked into the center comes out clean (about two hours). Serve the hot pudding at once.

*Serves* 8

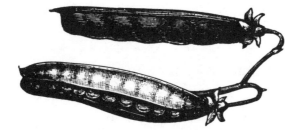

## Succotash Stew

✪

Succotash is an Indian word for a stew of corn and beans. The vegetables were sometimes cooked with bear meat, fat, or pieces of wild birds. The Pilgrims ate succotash often. This recipe makes a filling main dish.

INGREDIENTS

| | |
|---|---|
| ⅓ *cup dried lima beans* | 1 *pound stew meat* |
| *water* | 3 *tablespoons butter* |
| ½ *cup milk* | ½ *teaspoon salt* |
| ½ *cup water* | ¼ *teaspoon black pepper* |
| 2 *ears fresh corn* | ¼ *teaspoon cinnamon* |

1 • Put the dried lima beans in a one-and-a-half-quart pot. Cover them with cold water. Bring the water to a boil and boil for three minutes. Remove the pot from the heat, cover, and let it stand for one hour. Drain the beans. Cover them with fresh water. Bring to a boil. Reduce heat, cover, and simmer the beans until tender (about three minutes). Drain. Peel off and discard the skins. Set beans aside.

2 • Pour half a cup of milk and half a cup of water into a one-quart pot. Bring to a boil. While this mixture is heating to a boil, remove the husks and silk from the corn and throw them away. Cut off the kernels. Add the kernels to the boiling mixture of milk and water. Reduce the heat, cover, and simmer until the kernels are tender (about three minutes). Drain the kernels and set aside.

3 • Cut the stew meat into strips about one and a half inches long. Melt two tablespoons of butter in a heavy frying pan.

Add the meat and cook over medium heat, turning it to brown all sides. Sprinkle the meat with salt, black pepper, and cinnamon.

4 • Reduce the heat to low. Add one tablespoon butter. Gently stir in the cooked lima beans and corn. Continue to cook, stirring, until the vegetables are heated. Serve at once.

*Serves 4*

# Spicy Cucumber Catsup

✿

The Pilgrims loved spicy sauces. They made thick catsups out of grapes, squash, cucumbers, and even mushrooms.

### INGREDIENTS

4 *medium cucumbers*

*salt*

1 *small yellow onion*

3 *tablespoons white vinegar*

½ *teaspoon black pepper*

1 *tablespoon fresh dill, chopped*

1 • Wash the cucumbers. Pat dry. Peel off the skins with a vegetable peeler. Cut each cucumber lengthwise into four pieces. Remove and discard the seeds. Put the cucumbers in a glass bowl. Sprinkle lightly with salt and cover with cold water.

2 • Peel the onion. Cut it in half. Put it in a glass bowl and cover with cold water.

3 • Refrigerate cucumbers and onion for one hour.

4 • Drain cucumbers and onion. Grate them into a glass bowl. Sprinkle lightly with salt. Cover cucumber-onion mixture with plastic wrap and refrigerate it for two hours.

5 • Drain the mixture through a strainer. Press down with a fork to squeeze out all the water. Put the mixture back into the glass bowl. Add the vinegar, black pepper, and chopped dill.

6 • Place the mixture in the blender. Blend on low speed for two minutes. Pour into a one-pint glass jar and refrigerate for six hours.

*Makes one pint*

# Bannock Cakes

✿

Bannock cakes are easy to make. The Pilgrims had them at almost every meal. Try eating them hot, like pancakes, with butter and maple syrup.

Or put away your fork and eat them with your fingers the way the Pilgrims did.

### INGREDIENTS

1 *cup water*

1 *cup stone-ground cornmeal*

½ *teaspoon salt*

½ *cup milk*

1 *egg*

2 *tablespoons butter*

1 • Bring one cup of water to a boil.

2 • Mix the cornmeal and salt with a fork. Add the boiling water. Stir until the mixture is smooth. Stir in the milk. Let the batter sit for five minutes. Beat in the egg.

3 • Melt two tablespoons butter in a heavy frying pan over medium heat. Drop the batter from a tablespoon to make little round cakes. Cook the cakes until golden (about two minutes). Turn each cake with a spatula and cook the other side about one minute. Place the finished cakes on a serving platter. May be served either hot or cold.

*Serves 6*

# Whole Baked Pumpkin
# Stuffed with Apples

✪

We have pumpkin at morning
And pumpkin at noon;
If it was not for pumpkin,
We would be undoon.

—old rhyme

The Pilgrims ate lots of pumpkins. They ate pumpkin bread, pumpkin pudding, pumpkin pie, pumpkinseed cereal, and even pumpkin catsup. Sometimes they dried the pumpkin shell and used it as a dish.

## INGREDIENTS

1 *medium pumpkin*
*vegetable oil*

6 *small red apples*
*maple syrup*

1 • Preheat the oven to 350 degrees. Line a cookie sheet with aluminum foil.

2 • Wash the pumpkin in cold water. Pat dry. Cut a circle about four inches in diameter around the stem. Lift the stem and put the top aside. Scoop out and throw away the seeds and the soft pulp that sticks to them. Brush the outside of the pumpkin with vegetable oil.

3 • Wash the apples in cold water. Pat dry. Core the apples. Spoon one teaspoon of maple syrup into each apple. Carefully place the apples upright inside the pumpkin. Spoon two teaspoons of maple syrup over them. Replace the pumpkin top.

4 • Put the pumpkin on the cookie sheet and place it in the oven. Bake until the pumpkin and the apples are tender (one and a half to two hours).

5 • Remove the pumpkin from the oven. It will be very hot. Carefully remove the top. Take out the apples. Slice the pumpkin into six pieces. Put a piece of pumpkin and a baked apple on each plate. Pass a pitcher of maple syrup.

*Serves 6*

# Bearberry Jelly

❂

Cranberries were sometimes called bearberries because bears love to eat them.

## INGREDIENTS

1 *cup water*

2 *cups fresh cranberries*

2 *cups sugar*

1 *teaspoon cinnamon*

1 • Bring one cup of water to a boil.

2 • Put the cranberries in a colander. Rinse them with cold water. Throw away any berries that are dried out or mushy.

3 • Pour the cranberries into a heavy one-and-a-half-quart pot. Add the boiling water. Cook over medium heat until the berries pop (about three minutes).

4 • Press the berries and the cooking liquid through a strainer into a clean bowl.

5 • Pour the strained berry juice back into the pot. Bring it to a boil. Stir in the sugar. Boil, stirring occasionally, for five minutes. Remove from the heat. Skim off the foam with a wooden spoon. Stir in the cinnamon.

6 • Rinse out a glass jar with hot water. Pour in the berry mixture. Cover and chill. The jelly will be ready to eat in six hours.

*Makes three cups*

# Swizzle

❁

Swizzle is a cooling drink of water, vinegar, molasses, and spices. It is easy to prepare.

### INGREDIENTS

I *quart water*

¾ *cup molasses*

¼ *cup white vinegar*

½ *teaspoon ginger*

1 • Mix the ingredients in a glass jar. Shake them well.

2 • Refrigerate overnight. Serve cold.

*Serves 6–8*

# Hot Nuts

✸

Children liked this riddle:

> As soft as silk, as white as milk,
> As bitter as gall, a thick wall
> And a green coat covers me all.

The answer is a walnut.

Pilgrim children gathered nuts when they ripened and fell from the trees. Hot roasted nuts were a popular dessert, especially on winter evenings.

### INGREDIENTS

*2 cups of unshelled mixed nuts—walnuts,*
*hickory nuts, and hazelnuts*

1 • Preheat the oven to 400 degrees.

2 • Spread the nuts in one layer on a heavy cookie sheet. Bake in the oven for fifteen minutes.

3 • Remove from the oven. Put the nuts in a bowl. Give your guests plates and nutcrackers and invite them to help themselves to the hot nuts.

✿

These recipes are simple ones. They come from different times in Pilgrim history.

The Pilgrims may have prepared hot nuts as soon as their first fires burned down to ashes. But they made succotash stew only after they had harvested beans and corn, and after a successful hunt for wild animals or birds. It was probably served at the first Thanksgiving meal.

They made corn soup and pickled eggs during their first years in America. But they couldn't make sweet jellies and puddings until they began trading for maple syrup, sugar, and molasses.

With courage and hard work, the Pilgrims earned every change in their daily menu. No matter how hard their lives were, they never gave up. They ate their dry, buggy meals on the *Mayflower*. They snatched handfuls of berries and nuts to keep themselves going during the first hard years. And at last they were successful.

The children and grandchildren of the original Pilgrim settlers felt safe in America. They were eating hot, tasty food. They were never hungry. And they never forgot how much they owed their ancestors who had come on the *Mayflower*.

Today we still remember, and the achievement of the Pilgrims seems more remarkable every year.

Their voyage itself was an act of amazing courage. When the *Mayflower* sailed for America, the Pilgrims knew less about their destination than our astronauts did when they blasted off for the moon.

Once they arrived, their survival required heroism—not the astronaut's kind, but the kind that keeps ordinary people working at tasks beyond their strength. When we microwave a frozen pizza or pick up hamburgers at a drive-in, it's startling to think about the labor that every Pilgrim meal—every mouthful—required.

After you use these recipes to prepare a Pilgrim feast, as you're getting ready to take your first bite, close your eyes a moment to think of those brave men, women, and children who ate the same foods so long ago.

My story's ended,
My spoon is bended.
If you don't like it,
Go to the next door
And get it mended.

# Glossary

✺

*A word fitly spoken is like apples of gold
in a setting of silver.*

—Proverbs  25:11

*Andirons* • A pair of iron stands used for holding logs in the fire-place.

*Bake Kettle* • A three-legged covered iron pot that stood right in the fire. Hot ashes were shoveled onto the cover to help the food cook quickly.

*Bannock Cake* • Small, flat breads cooked on a griddle.

*Betty Lamp* • A little metal dish in which fish oil was burned to provide light.

*Black Jack* • A drinking cup made out of boiled leather.

*Bread Peel* • A flat wooden shovel used to slide loaves of bread in and out of the oven.

*Burgoo* • A boiled gruel of hot oatmeal and molasses.

*Charger* • A large, round platter on which food was brought to the table.

*Cider* • A drink made from mashed apples.

*Cooper* • A barrel maker.

*Doughboys* • Bits of wet flour fried in pork fat.

*Firebox* • A small iron box, half-filled with sand, in which cooking fires were made aboard ships.

*Hall* • The main room in most Pilgrim houses. Used for cooking, eating, sleeping, working, and playing.

*Hasty Pudding* • A pudding made by boiling flour and water in a cloth bag.

*Herbs* • The name the Pilgrims used for all leafy vegetables.

*Hoecakes* • Little round cakes made of flour and water and baked on the blade of a hoe, which was stuck into the hot ashes at the edge of a fire.

*Hogshead* • A large barrel in which cider was stored.

*Hominy* • A cereal made by grinding and boiling the soft insides of corn kernels.

*Horsebread* • A coarse bread made from ground peas. Sometimes fed to the pigs.

*Johnnycakes* • Small, flat cakes made of cornmeal and water. Often carried by Pilgrim travelers.

*Labscouse* • A soup made with spices, dried peas, salted beef, and water.

*Latchkey* • A wooden peg at the end of a string, used for pulling up the latch to open a door.

*Lug Pole* • A thick, green wood pole mounted above the fireplace. Used to hang pots and kettles directly over the flames.

*Musket* • A large, heavy handgun with a long barrel like a rifle.

*Neat's Tongue* • A dried ox tongue.

*Noggin* • An eight-sided cup with a handle.

*Pap* • A mixture of milk and flour that was the first food Pilgrim babies ate.

*Peachy* • A drink made from the juice of mashed peaches.

*Perry* • A drink made from the juice of mashed pears.

*Pewter* • A metal made by melting tin together with lead or copper. The Pilgrims used plates and cups made of pewter.

*Pilgrim* • A person who travels to a faraway place to pray there. The English settlers who founded Plymouth Colony were all called Pilgrims.

*Plum Duff* • A fatty pudding made with raisins or dried prunes.

*Root Cellar* • An underground cellar used for storing vegetables, barrels of pickled meat, and preserves.

*Roots* • Vegetables that grow underground, like carrots.

*Rushlight* • A light made by sticking one end of a rush—a thick, hollow grass—into hot animal fat and setting the fat on fire.

*Rye 'n Injun* • Bread made from a mixture of ground Indian corn and rye flour.

*Sallet* • Salad.

*Sawyer* • A worker who saws lumber into planks.

*Settle* • A long wooden bench with arms and a high back.

*Ship's Biscuit* • A large, round, hard biscuit made of flour and water, eaten by sailors and passengers on ships.

*Spit* • A pointed iron rod used to hold a roast above a fire and turn it.

*Spoon Meat* • Any cooked food that is eaten with a spoon, like pudding.

*Tankard* • A cup with a hinged top.

*Tanner* • A worker who cures animal skins.

*Trencher* • A dish made from wood or stale bread.

*Trundle Bed* • A small bed stored under a larger one and pulled out to be used.

*Voider* • A basket passed around at mealtime to collect the dirty dishes and utensils.

*Warming Pan* • A long-handled copper pan filled with hot coals. Passed back and forth under the bed covers to warm them.

*White Pot* • A custard made of baked eggs and milk.

# Selected Bibliography

Bradford, William. *Of Plymouth Plantation*. New York: Alfred A. Knopf, 1952.

Caffrey, Kate. *The Mayflower*. New York: Stein and Day, 1974.

Cowie, Leonard W. *The Pilgrim Fathers*. New York: G. P. Putnam's Sons, 1970.

Earle, Alice Morse. *Customs and Fashions in Old New England*. New York: Charles Scribner's Sons, 1898.

Gill, Crispin. *Mayflower Remembered: A History of the Plymouth Pilgrims*. New York: Taplinger Publishing Company, 1970.

Gould, Mary Earle. *The Early American House*. Rutland, Vermont: Charles E. Tuttle Company, Inc., 1949.

Hole, Christina. *English Home-Life 1500 to 1800*. London and New York: B. T. Batsford Ltd., 1947.

Kimball, Yeffe, and Jean Anderson. *The Art of American Indian Cooking*. New York: Simon and Schuster, 1965.

Langdon, William Chancy. *Everyday Things in American Life, 1607–1776*. New York: Charles Scribner's Sons, 1937.

Rickert, Edith, tr. *The Babee's Book: Medieval Manners for the Young*. New York and London: Chatto and Windus, 1908.

Rutman, Darrett B. *Husbandmen of Plymouth: Farms and Villages in the Old Colony, 1620–1692.* Boston: Beacon Press, 1967.

Train, Arthur. *The Story of Everyday Things.* New York and London: Harper and Brothers, Publishers, 1941.

Tunis, Edwin. *Colonial Living.* Cleveland and New York: The World Publishing Company, 1957.

Willison, George F. *Saints and Strangers.* New York: Reynal and Hitchcock, 1945.

Wilson, Everett B. *America's Vanishing Folkways.* New York: A. S. Barnes and Company, 1965.

# Index

❂

PICTURE CREDITS: p. iv, pp. 40-41 courtesy of the Abby Aldrich Rockefeller Folk Art Center, Williamsburg, Virginia; pp.6, 14. 44 courtesy of the Pilgrim Society, Plymouth, Massachusetts; p. 18 courtesy of the National Archives of Canada; p. 21 courtsey of the Peabody Museum of Salem; pp. 22, 88 by permission of the Massachusetts Historical Society; p. 25 courtesy of the Essex Institute, Salem, Massachusetts; p. 32 courtesy of Plymoth Plantation; p. 54 courtesy of the New York Historical Society, New York City; p. 72 courtesy of the Fine Arts Museums of San Francisco; p. 79 courtesy of the Worcester Art Museum, Worcester, Massachusetts.